Original title:
Sprouts of Silence

Copyright © 2025 Creative Arts Management OÜ
All rights reserved.

Author: Arabella Whitmore
ISBN HARDBACK: 978-1-80567-041-4
ISBN PAPERBACK: 978-1-80567-121-3

Silent Conversations with the Soil

In the hush where roots confide,
The earth shares secrets far and wide.
Worms giggle as they wiggle through,
Making jokes that only they construe.

The daisies whisper, 'Hey, look here!'
A breeze rolls in, a ticklish cheer.
Beetles chuckle at the flower's prance,
Creating chaos in a silent dance.

The Beauty of Muted Colors

In shadows where the hues do blend,
A lavender plot has got a bend.
The gray grass boasts of its own flair,
While violet petals flirt with air.

The smirk of moss on a tree's side,
In a world where giggles do reside.
Bumbling bees flaunt their fuzzy coats,
In laughter, even nature floats.

Beneath the Canopy of Quiet

Under the green where whispers dwell,
A squirrel shares tales it won't quite tell.
The leaves lean in, hushed with glee,
Each branch joins in, a comedy spree.

The shadows stretch and play a game,
With sunlight laughing at their fame.
Pillows of clover tease the ground,
Making soft jests without a sound.

The Gentle Stir of Life

Where life stirs with a cheeky grin,
A budding bloom tosses its chin.
The wind tickles every stem around,
As nature giggles without a sound.

Tiny critters plotting their schemes,
With winks exchanged amid the beams.
In the calm, mischief takes a ride,
In the light, jests bloom side by side.

The Calm Before the Growth

In the garden, whispers play,
Beneath the ground, they jig and sway.
Ants march like they own the show,
While worms just giggle, 'here we grow!'

Sunlight winks, the breeze it struts,
In a dance that tickles roots and guts.
Each seed's a joker, full of jest,
Waiting for rain to feast its quest.

Secrets Beneath the Soil

In the quiet, secrets churn,
With tiny gales, the roots take turns.
Grapes are betting on a plump win,
While carrots hide, afraid of thin skin.

Moles in shades, wearing tiny caps,
Plotting their paths, avoiding mishaps.
Beans are snoozing, but still they scheme,
Dreaming of heights and sunlit beams.

Veils of Motionless Life

Underneath a cloak of earth,
Lies a joke that's full of mirth.
Bulbs are chuckling, hiding tight,
Biding time for their big debut night.

Silly sprouts, so shy yet bold,
Under the stars, their tales unfold.
Each root a prankster, laughter stored,
Poking the sky, like laughter poured.

Threads of Muffled Echoes

In hushed tones, a giggle swells,
As roots play tag with soil-bound spells.
Frogs croak jokes, in silent queues,
Nature's humor, no need for cues.

Leaves chime softly with loose delight,
Tickling the air, what a sight!
Whispers bounce like tiny balls,
While ladybugs share tea, and giggle in lulls.

Listening to the Silence

In a room full of chatter,
The clock ticks a little patter.
I think I heard a potato snore,
Should I laugh or just ignore?

The walls are wearing quiet socks,
While mice hold a party with their clocks.
A whispering breeze tells a joke,
And the curtains giggle, what a poke!

The Lullaby of Leaves

The leaves sing softly of dreams and cheer,
They plot how to tickle the next passerby here.
With a rustle and shake, they wiggle away,
Making the squirrels join in the play.

Branches do cartwheels, what a sight,
Winking at breezes as they twirl and flight.
Each acorn a drummer in leafy disguise,
While the toadstools tap dance and rise.

Subtle Whispers of Dawn

As dawn creeps in with sleepy eyes,
The coffee pot sings its morning lies.
Birds chirp gossip that's hard to believe,
About a worm that dared to eavesdrop, I retrieve!

The sun yawns wide, stretching its rays,
And the shadows dance in a silly ballet.
Every blade of grass cracks a joke,
While the first light winks, it's no hoax.

Embracing the Unseen

Invisible friends have a hoot and a laugh,
Debating if shadows deserve a photograph.
They change forms in a whimsy parade,
Tickling the air, but never displayed.

A giggle escapes from the corner of dark,
As fireflies join with a luminous spark.
The moon, in on it, throws a sly grin,
As night plays a prank, let the fun begin!

Muted Harmonies

Whispers dance on tip-toe feet,
Eggplants giggle, tomatoes greet.
Lettuce leans to share a joke,
As carrots take a joyful poke.

Beans in shades of green so bright,
Crack up nightly under moonlight.
The cucumbers chuckle, don't you see?
Their laughter grows, oh so carefree!

Peace in the Understory

In the moss, a cautious snail,
Dares to dance, it leaves a trail.
Fungus giggles, 'What a sight!'
Toadstools blush in pure delight.

The bunnies in their little huddle,
Debate the merits of a cuddle.
While crickets tune their finest strings,
Contemplating the joy that spring brings.

Stillness Unveiled

Amidst the pines, a whisper came,
Squirrels playing their nutty game.
Breezes tease with silly signs,
While shadows mimic tangled lines.

A fox in shades of orange fame,
Winks at the world without a shame.
Leaves rustle as if to laugh,
As nature takes its bubbly path.

Awakening Shadows

As dawn creeps in with golden rays,
A hedgehog snoozes through the plays.
Chirping birds, their jokes so grand,
Invite the worms to join the band.

An owl hoots, but just for fun,
While mushrooms plot their morning run.
The dance begins beneath the trees,
Where laughter floats upon the breeze.

Stillness in Bloom

In the garden where whispers play,
The daisies have much to say.
They giggle as the breezes laugh,
And share their tales in a soft path.

The roses blush with a secret tease,
While turtles dance with clumsy ease.
The sunbeams join in a playful race,
As shadows hide with a smiling face.

Graceful Growth

The beans have dreams of being high,
While carrots watch and wonder why.
They plan a party beneath the moon,
With veggies swaying to a leafy tune.

The radishes hop in their tight red coats,
Telling jokes about curious goats.
Lettuce giggles, feeling quite green,
At how the world is a lively scene.

The Soft Caress of Time

Time tiptoes through the forest floor,
Tickling leaves, always wanting more.
The squirrels chuckle at its gentle pace,
As sunshine dances in its warm embrace.

Bubbles of laughter rise from the brook,
While fish tell tales in their secret nook.
Moss collects giggles like jewels so fine,
As hours bloom in a whimsical line.

Nature's Softest Secrets

The whispers of ferns in a secret plot,
Tell tales of dances that time forgot.
The stars join in with a twinkling grin,
While crickets compose a night's violin.

Dewdrops giggle on petals at dawn,
Painting the world with a soft yawn.
Even the rocks have a chuckle, it seems,
As they snooze under the weight of their dreams.

Threads of Peace

In a garden where whispers grow,
The tomatoes debate the status quo.
Carrots chuckle as they dig,
While onions cry, but that's their gig.

The lettuce dances, all a-flutter,
While peppers giggle, 'Oh, what a clutter!'
Radishes joke, 'We're the roots of fun!'
In this green world, peace weighs a ton.

The cucumbers wander, looking for light,
"Who needs a sun?" they giggle at night.
Zucchini grins, with a wink so sly,
"Don't be so green, just give it a try!"

As sprouts take center stage, they cheer,
In this land of silence, laughter is near.
Nature's bounty speaks this way,
It's funny to see the plants at play.

The Soundless Bounty of Nature

In the quiet woods, a squirrel pranced,
Up the tree, quite under-chanced.
With acorns stacked in silly piles,
He grinned wide, sharing his winks and smiles.

Mushrooms giggle in their fungal beds,
They swap jokes with the leaves overhead.
"Why did the leaf blush?" they shout with glee,
"Because it saw the tree's bare knee!"

Foxes scamper, tails in a twirl,
While crickets hold a night-time whirl.
They chirp about all the fun they had,
And laugh so loud, it'd make you glad.

A band of owls on a branch did convene,
They discuss nonsense, all serene.
In this echo of peace, where no sound rings,
Nature's bounty knows laughter brings.

Silence Wrapped in Green

In the garden, whispers play,
Leaves are gossiping all day.
Squirrels pause with tiny grins,
Listening where the laughter spins.

Beneath the blooms, a secret lies,
A frog croaks jokes; oh how it flies!
Dancing daisies take a leap,
While shy tulips settle deep.

Nature's Softest Echoes

Petals tickle in the breeze,
Bumblebees wear polka peas.
Clouds above begin to jest,
Making shadows play the best.

With each rustle, trees confide,
Birch trees laugh, while pines collide.
The whispers weave a silly tale,
As squirrels debate who will prevail.

Spoken in Silence

A snail slides by, a slow parade,
While flowers giggle in the shade.
Beetles pop their tiny tags,
And ladybugs wear funky rags.

Chirping crickets offer puns,
Dandelions share their buns.
Nature's chat, both sly and sweet,
Leaves us longing for another seat.

Growth Within the Quiet

Mushrooms sport their polka dots,
While hidden roots share funny thoughts.
The earth chuckles 'neath our feet,
As grass declares it won the heat.

Underneath the compost pile,
Worms exchange a wiggly smile.
With each sprout that daintily creeps,
The humor of the soil runs deep.

Silent Entanglements

In the garden, whispers grow,
Beneath the soil, secrets flow.
Worms waltz in a silent spree,
Telling jokes to the bumblebee.

A cactus laughs, its spikes a grin,
While mushrooms giggle, thick and thin.
The daisies dance in quiet cheer,
Waiting for a chatty deer.

Roots entwined in tangled jest,
Nature plays, it knows what's best.
A leaf sneezes with a soundless flair,
And daisies wink at the froggy stare.

In this realm of hush and fun,
Nature's comedy has just begun.
Each bloom and blade has tales to tell,
In a world where silence casts its spell.

Life's Quiet Genesis

Tiny seeds in a hushed ballet,
Poking heads up to greet the day.
With a soft yawn, the sun appears,
As laughter echoes in hushed cheers.

Gentle breezes tickle the air,
Grass blades giggle without a care.
A beetle slips, he tries to boast,
But all that's heard's a silent toast.

In corners where shadows softly play,
Mice tell stories, but not today.
They're wrapped in plots of leafy schemes,
Caught up in silent, pastel dreams.

Each sprout emerges, bold and meek,
In whispers they trade the grandest cheek.
With roots that twist like playful puns,
The earth laughs low, as life's begun.

Pastel Dreams of the Earth

Colors bloom where quiet stands,
Pastels paint the slumbering lands.
A shy petal blushes with delight,
As butterflies wear socks too tight.

With every hue that softly sleeps,
Nature plays hide and seek in peeps.
A robin chuckles at the hues,
Singing songs to the morning dew.

In laughter's grip, the colors sway,
Remembering what flowers say.
The earth spins tales, both loud and meek,
While in the silence, it's all unique.

Jumping jays with feathers bright,
Stumble in a funny flight.
In every shade of quiet fun,
The pastel dreams just weigh a ton.

The Hidden Palette of Nature

In silence, colors start to scheme,
Nature's palette hides a dream.
Brushes made from squirrel's tails,
Sketching stories where laughter trails.

A wandering breeze, a whiff of cat,
Watch out for that sleepy bat!
As petals wink, all secrets show,
Muted jokes in the winds that blow.

A dandelion puffs in jest,
Sending wishes, feeling blessed.
With whispers carried from leaf to leaf,
Nature giggles behind our grief.

So let us waltz through shades unseen,
In this vivid yet quiet scene.
Where laughter blooms and silence plays,
The hidden hues brightening our days.

Traces of a Distant Whisper

In the garden where giggles play,
Plants gossip about the sunny day.
They chuckle at bees with their silly dance,
Until a breeze gives them all a chance.

Leaves murmur secrets, all in good fun,
While roots plot mischief under the sun.
A worm tells jokes that make flowers grin,
And laughter erupts from a poor old din.

Stones roll their eyes at chatter so spry,
Giving looks that make daisies sigh.
Oh, to be part of the soil's sweet jest,
Where nonsense blooms, and silence is blessed.

From shadows, whispers of giggles arise,
With humor that dances beneath bright skies.
Nature's awesome, with laughter to share,
In quiet corners, joy lurks everywhere.

Soft Blossoms of Contemplation

Petals ponder, pondering pink,
What's the best way for flowers to sync?
A daisy suggests a polite little bow,
While tulips debate their fashion somehow.

Sunflowers smile with a twist of their head,
Claiming they shine where others just dread.
They jest about clouds, so fluffy and bold,
Trading puns with the daisies, young and old.

The breeze, a jester, floats through the patch,
Tickling the buds to help them hatch.
Lilies giggle at the stumbles they see,
Reveling in mishaps of bumblebee glee.

Nature's a jokester, in her subtle ways,
Creating a stage for whimsical plays.
In quiet hum, where thoughts grow unwound,
Laughter and whispers are perfectly bound.

Silence in Bloom

In the stillness, petals conspire,
To craft their own bloom of comic fire.
A rose cracks jokes, though it might prick,
Leaving us giggling from a floral trick.

The daffodils dance with a hop and a skip,
While violets tease from a lowly tip.
A shy little bud makes her first remark,
Sending ripples of humor through the dark.

In this garden of giggles, solitude sings,
Where quietness reigns and humor springs.
The whispers of joy, tangled in vines,
Create a soft laughter, as nature aligns.

Grazing on whimsy, the flowers conjoin,
A humorous league—oh, what a groin!
In a still moment, they share the delight,
Of mischief that blooms without any plight.

The Quiet Pulse of Nature

Underneath the surface, a chuckle is heard,
As crickets chirp with each splendid word.
They swap little tales about moonlit quests,
While owls drop puns, and they can't take rests.

In mossy beds where the toads like to leap,
They gather round to hear secrets they keep.
One toad jabs at the frogs in a jest,
While the lily pads giggle, oh what a fest!

The gentle wind laughs through branches above,
Sharing sweet whispers that float like a dove.
Nature's a clown, in a quirky ballet,
Enticing the silence to join in the play.

From roots to the sky, the humor does weave,
In the stillest of places, it's hard to believe.
As nature unravels its whimsical grace,
We find laughter's bloom in this quiet space.

Petals of Thoughtful Silence

In gardens where whispers play,
The bees are busy, making hay.
But did you hear the flowers speak?
They giggle softly, quite unique.

One rose said, "I'm more than bright!"
While daisies danced in pure delight.
Lilies blush when no one's near,
Their secrets shared, but not a peer.

The tulip told a joke so sly,
And even cacti laughed nearby.
In the quiet, humor grows,
Among the petals, joy bestows.

So when you walk through blooms so fair,
Listen close, there's laughter there.
In quiet moments, laughter blooms,
As petals chuckle in their rooms.

The Unseen Flourish

In shadows where the silence creeps,
The grass just laughs, while the silence weeps.
A dandelion plans to roam,
With dreams that wander far from home.

The mushrooms hold a secret jam,
Pasta sauce from a crafty ham.
Butterflies in bow ties fray,
As whispers tease the light of day.

Each leaf has tales of glee and woe,
When no one's near they put on a show.
Wait for the breeze, it tells the jest,
And nature's quirks are simply best.

So if you think it's quiet here,
Just lend an ear, and you may hear,
The rustling grass, the chirps that blend,
A symphony, where giggles send.

Timeless Murmurs

In corners where the shadows sway,
The crickets joke at end of day.
As stars align in quiet cheers,
They whisper tales from yesteryears.

The moon chuckles, bright and round,
While trees sway gently, making sound.
A squirrel giggles, what a sight,
As it prepares for fun-filled night.

The brook hums softly, clear and bright,
And pebbles snicker in their flight.
With whispers carried on the breeze,
Laughter dances, ticks like keys.

In silent moments, humor brews,
As echoes laugh and softly muse.
Listen close, the world insists,
Even quiet can't resist.

Quiet Revelations

In silence, secrets find their way,
A grasshopper cracks jokes all day.
With every hop, more laughter spills,
As nature crafts its playful thrills.

The willow bends to hear a tale,
Of snails who dream of setting sail.
And ants discuss their grand parade,
While counting crumbs they've carefully laid.

Oh, daisies blush at whispers sweet,
As bumblebees dance on tiny feet.
The wind composes soft haikus,
A comedic blend of nature's views.

So when you ponder, pause a bit,
Nature's laughter, not to omit.
In quiet realms, joy's never dense,
Funny vibes are just common sense.

Trapped in the Quietude

In hushed corners, whispers play,
Like ninja cats stalking the day.
Thoughts bounce off walls like ping-pong,
Who knew silence could feel so wrong?

My thoughts tango in a quiet jam,
While the kettle hums a secret spam.
Laughter hides beneath the bed,
Too shy to peek, so it stays unsaid.

Awakening in Muted Tones

The coffee pot sings a sleepy song,
While toast pops up with a cheerful prong.
Even the clock tickles its hands,
Trying to wake sleepy bands.

Muffins giggle on the kitchen rack,
Scones just sigh, feeling off track.
In muted shades of buttery cheer,
Even silence seems to disappear!

Delicate Pulse of Life

The plants are plotting a green parade,
With leaves that gossip in the shade.
Flowers burst into snickers and jest,
As dandelions play at being the best.

Bees hum softly, making the rounds,
Tickling blooms without making sounds.
Even the breeze tries to stifle a laugh,
As nature embraces its own autograph.

The Unseen Garden

In a garden where giggles sprout,
With daisies holding their blooms about.
The soil whispers secrets of mirth,
As worms wiggle, claiming their worth.

A gopher's peek raises a laugh,
Clumsy florals are on the path.
Sunbeams wink from the leafy cover,
In this quiet place, rhythm goes undercover.

Tranquil Tendrils

In the garden where whispers creep,
The carrots giggle, they just can't keep.
Radishes chuckle, trying to hide,
While cabbages dance with leafy pride.

Basil dreams of a tightrope walk,
Tomatoes chime in with cheeky talk.
The marigolds burst out in laughter,
While beans plot mischief, their happy chatter.

A potato slips on its own green bag,
Squeaking a sound as it begins to lag.
The onions wink with tears of joy,
As pumpkins jest, that cheeky ploy.

So gather 'round for jokes from dirt,
In this quirky realm, not a single hurt.
Each seedling tells stories with glee,
In this murmuring world, come and see!

Echoes in the Garden

In a patch where giggles sprout,
The peas are making quite a rout.
While lettuce whispers to the breeze,
"Don't ask the weeds, they won't appease."

Bees buzz in on the pun parade,
As flowers join, their worries fade.
A sunflower tips its hat so wide,
While radishes roll, with joy they slide.

The tomatoes blush, with just a tease,
As ants perform their acrobatic squeeze.
The rain drops grumble, but the leaves just sway,
In laughter's echo, they dance and play.

So stroll on through this cheerful maze,
Where every bloom is in a funny phase.
Roots tickle softly beneath our feet,
In this garden, silliness is a treat.

Tread Lightly Among the Blossoms

Tiptoe through blooms with a giggly sound,
Where the daisies gossip, oh what a crowd!
Laughter springs from the tulip's lip,
While violets play silly friendship trips.

Snapdragons snap with a playful cheer,
As bunnies hop close, drawing near.
The grasses sway in a merry dance,
While ladybugs spin in a funky trance.

A worm cracks jokes under the soil,
With every chuckle, true laughter uncoils.
The daisies swoon, feeling so spry,
While butterflies flutter, floating high.

So tread with care, but feel the glee,
Among the blossoms, run wild and free.
Each petal whispers a funny thought,
In this bloom-filled place, happiness is caught.

The Soft Starting Place

In the corner of the garden bright,
The seedlings plot till late at night.
Carrots whisper, "You won't believe,"
How they plan to take over and deceive!

The mint makes jokes, fresh as can be,
While herbs roll around beneath the trees.
Tomatoes giggle, they've got good style,
As radishes stomp with a cheeky smile.

Pansies ponder on life's great quest,
While daisies prep for a silly fest.
With every sunbeam, laughter grows,
Echoing softly, as everyone knows.

So welcome to this playful space,
Where laughter wraps around each face.
Nature's humor, both wild and spry,
In the soft starting place, let's laugh and fly!

Echoes in the Stillness

In the kitchen, pots do chatter,
While the cat holds court, a nimble batter.
The fridge hums with secrets untold,
And the clock ticks, a story unfolds.

Whispers glide on the evening air,
While my socks dance without a care.
The ceiling fan does a wobbly spin,
As the vacuum's grumble begins to grin.

A cooing dove on a telephone wire,
Spreads gossip about the yard's attire.
The dog barks at shadows on the wall,
While I snicker at my own miscall.

In the quiet, laughter finds its place,
As I search for my keys with a warm embrace.
The world hums a tune we can't quite hear,
In the stillness, the giggles draw near.

Seeds of Serenity

In the meadow, ants hold a parade,
Marching while dodging the shadows they've made.
The daisies gossip, all dressed in white,
Tickling the grass, quaking with delight.

A squirrel hops with an acorn in tow,
While the wind whispers soft, "Go with the flow."
The clouds tease the sun, playing hide and seek,
Frolicsome they are, quite cheeky, not meek.

Butterflies giggle, flitting about,
Daring each petal to dance, flout, and sprout.
While frogs compose tunes with a croaky flair,
And crickets play chess in the cool evening air.

In the hush where the breezes purr,
Even the brook has a story to blur.
Nature's own jesters, on laughter they thrive,
In this calm, the funny keeps us alive.

Gardens of the Unspoken

In the garden, carrots tickle each toe,
While tomatoes plot their famous throw.
The corn reaches for stars, all in a row,
And the beans have plans, oh, the seeds they sow.

A scarecrow grins with straw-stuffed pride,
As butterflies dance, side by side.
Sunflowers peek from their leafy retreat,
Throwing shade while the daisies compete.

The moles have meetings beneath the ground,
While worms wiggle, a clever sound.
The roses gossip on scents so sweet,
In this quiet, the giggles discreet.

As night wraps the garden in velvet dreams,
Soft laughter rises beside the moonbeams.
In the hush, where nature tends to play,
Funny little secrets sneak in to stay.

Murmurs of the Earth

The earth chuckles, a soft, rolling sound,
As the wind whispers tales, swirling around.
A rabbit with ears perked, listen well,
To the stories that tumble within each shell.

The puddles reflect both laughter and light,
While shadows do dances, quite out of sight.
Frogs serenade owls with a playful croon,
While the crickets compose a puntastic tune.

A tumbleweed rolls through the scene at dusk,
Adding a twist where the air holds its musk.
Beneath the stars, secrets tickle the air,
And the night holds a charm that's funny, yet rare.

In the echoes of earth, giggles abound,
Where each little whisper is joyfully found.
Nature's own chuckles, a sound that won't cease,
In the quiet, humor whispers, bringing peace.

Shadows of Serenity

In corners where shadows play,
Dancing gnomes hold sway.
With tickles from the breeze,
They spill secrets with ease.

The squirrels giggle and chatter,
Odd tales that just don't matter.
Who knew trees could nod and wink?
I swear, they love to think!

While sunlight peeks and blinks,
The daisies laugh, or so it thinks.
A grasshopper steals the show,
With a limbo dance, oh so slow!

In stillness, mischief brews,
With whispers of silly news.
Rainbows flee from too much hush,
As the garden tries to rush!

Seeds Beneath the Surface

Beneath the ground, a plot unfolds,
Where gossipy roots share stories untold.
They chuckle as they wiggle and squirm,
While carrots plot their own hilarious term.

A lettuce leaf thinks it's quite the sage,
Teasing sprouts like a friendly mage.
"Let's play hide and seek!" it shouts,
But the radish just snores—what a bout!

Potatoes roll their eyes for fun,
Claiming they've got the hard work done.
Yet the peas sing their sweet runtime,
In a symphony so out of rhyme!

Oh, the fun that life can hold,
In quiet plots, so bold.
Silly seeds, with laughter rife,
Each day's a party, full of life!

The Hush of Hidden Growth

In the dark where giggles creep,
Beneath the soil, secrets sleep.
The mushrooms share a stew of dreams,
While worms combine their silly schemes.

Roots tickle with tiny, secret glows,
As daisies plot their funny shows.
"Why did the sprout cross the lane?"
"To tell a joke and entertain!"

The daffodils sway with laughter's shine,
Poking fun at the sun's decline.
While others whisper, 'Shh, be still,'
The garden giggles, and it's a thrill!

Chuckles hide in the silent lush,
In the chaos of a gentle hush.
Nature's comedy, raw and true,
In every leaf, a giggle grew!

Murmurs of the Unsaid

In the hush, whispers twirl about,
"Did you hear what that beet said out?"
A tulip giggles, a little keen,
"Only if it's not too obscene!"

The daisies whisper behind their backs,
Making notes on shady tracks.
"We're so stealthy, can't you see?
A garden's gossip is truly key!"

Thistles roll their prickly eyes,
Yet join in on all the sly replies.
Beneath the laughter, secrets churn,
And every quiet plant has much to learn.

From roots to blooms, tales are spun,
Puns blooming in the warming sun.
So let's unearth the silent cheer,
Where blooms bring laughter year to year!

Breaths Between Moments

In a world of endless chatter,
The whispers dance, a jovial matter.
Squirrels gossip, trees have a laugh,
While clouds chuckle on their sunny path.

Breezes tease the daisies bright,
Tickling petals, taking flight.
The pine trees sway with giddy grace,
Nature's jesters in a leafy place.

The shadows giggle, hiding away,
While crickets play their night ballet.
A frog croaks jokes from his lily throne,
Every croak a chuckle, all alone.

In this lighthearted, silent space,
Joy takes root in every nook and place.
Moments of mirth, so soft and spry,
Life's great comedy, passing by.

Hidden Harmonies of Reflection

In puddles of laughter, frogs take a dive,
Ripples vibrating, keeping dreams alive.
Reflections giggle in the morning dew,
As flowers share secrets only they knew.

The willow weeps, but don't be dismayed,
Her tears are simply jokes she's made.
While bees in their buzz create a song,
Nature's choir where all belong.

A bumblebee stings with humor untold,
Dancing around flowers, feeling bold.
In gardens where silence colors the air,
Every leaf has a tale to share.

Through the lens of a breeze, a laughter unfurls,
Like squirrels trading stories, oh the swirls!
These hidden harmonies stir the day,
In quiet chuckles, they all play.

The Stillness of Blossoming

In the stillness where petals unfold,
Laughter rises, quiet and bold.
Buds crack jokes, blooming with flair,
Each blossom a punchline, quite rare.

Bumblebees buzz with sticky delight,
Wings a-flutter, taking flight.
The fragrance of humor fills the air,
As daisies wink, without a care.

Though whispers linger, let them play,
In this stillness, a joyful ballet.
Around every stem where shadows dance,
Nature invites you to take a chance.

In silence, soft glee blossoms anew,
Colors erupt in laughter's hue.
From quiet depths, the fun begins,
In every rustle, nature grins.

Nature's Silent Rebirth

In whispers of spring, the pranks reappear,
Funny little creatures frolic near.
The earth chuckles, shaking off snow,
As daffodils giggle, putting on a show.

From hidden corners, laughter erupts,
A rabbit slips by, hops, and erupts.
While trees doze off, dreaming of pranks,
Nature's critters filling the banks.

Each petal that opens shares a quick grin,
As worms tell tales beneath the skin.
The rivers hum tunes, bubbling with cheer,
In the stillness of life, the fun draws near.

With every dawn, there's a laugh renewed,
The earth's rebirth, a joyous mood.
In silence, the world finds a fresh start,
With nature's mirth, it steals our heart.

The Subtle Symphony of Existence

In a world where whispers play,
Even clumsy frogs find their way.
Each giggle hides a larger scheme,
As ants conspire beneath the cream.

Tickling grass, a secret plot,
The trees engage in chatter hot.
A snail's slow dance, a graceful jest,
While petals giggle in their rest.

Crickets chirp their witty lines,
As shadows dance on wobbly pines.
The breeze tickles with a wry grin,
Unseen mischief under the skin.

Amidst the chaos, calm prevails,
As nature's humor softly trails.
In this symphony, we play along,
With giggles woven in the throng.

Gardens of Implied Words

In gardens where the daisies snicker,
And tulips blush, just a tad quicker.
They gossip softly about the bees,
Rumbling under the dappled trees.

A rumor sprouts among the vines,
That carrots mock the potato lines.
While leafy greens play hide and seek,
And cucumbers wear a coat of chic.

The roses chuckle, oh so bright,
As veggies argue about who's right.
In this patch, where secrets unfold,
The silence speaks, and the laughter's bold.

Such jesters hiding in plain sight,
As sunlight dances, pure delight.
Each bloom a comic, a tale to tell,
In a garden where mirth does dwell.

Whispers Beneath the Soil

Down below, the roots convene,
Whiskers twitch in shades of green.
They gossip 'bout the ants' parade,
And giggles echo in the glade.

Earthworms wiggle, a squirmy dance,
Plotting pranks with every chance.
While buried seeds send out a laugh,
As sprouts prepare for their autograph.

Rabbits lend an ear to tune,
As moles debate with tiny brooms.
A hidden world of jests unfurled,
In the stillness, joy's twirled.

Nature's humor, soft and shy,
Permeates as time drifts by.
In the hush of earth's embrace,
Laughter blossoms, takes its place.

Budding Quietude

In quietude, the puns take flight,
As buds prepare to greet the light.
A bashful bloom gets ready to pose,
Whispering secrets to all that grows.

The daisies trip on their own feet,
While violets compete for the sweetest seat.
Sunflowers boast with a towering view,
As laughter sneaks in the morning dew.

Quiet moments, yet blooms proclaim,
Their petals softened with subtle shame.
Each breeze brings whispers, a gentle tease,
Where joy and silence dance with ease.

In this still air, let chuckles flow,
From every garden, a playful show.
With nature's charm, we all unite,
In a budding world, just pure delight.

Gentle Cradles of Life

In a pot, a plant took a nap,
Dreaming of soil, like a cozy lap.
Worms doing yoga, oh what a sight,
Sipping on dew, feeling just right.

Bugs host a party, they all bring snacks,
Dancing on leaves, avoiding the cracks.
While raindrops giggle, they pop and they play,
Making mud pies in a wiggly way.

Roots whisper secrets beneath the ground,
As ants write letters, oh what a sound!
Squirrels tell jokes, with acorns in tow,
Life is a circus, just watch it all grow.

Each day brings laughter in the still air,
Nature's own theater, no need for a chair.
With flowers on stage, they burst into cheer,
In this leafy world, there's nothing to fear.

Unheard Songs of Green

The grass hums softly, though none can hear,
Tickling each toe, brings laughter and cheer.
Crickets compose, their symphonies bold,
While daisies comment, they'd never be sold.

Frogs in the pond croak out their tunes,
While fish in the water dance under moons.
Beetles rock out on a leaf-turned-stage,
And caterpillars read from an ancient page.

Trees share tall tales, with leaves all aglow,
Each whisper a secret from long ago.
Sunshine and shadows throw in their part,
In a world full of giggles, each beat is a heart.

So raise up your voice, join this silent parade,
And twirl with the flowers in colors displayed.
For in every rustle, a chuckle is found,
In this vibrant realm, joy knows no bound.

Echoing Hues of Calm

The sky paints laughter in pastel delights,
With clouds that giggle on soft, fluffy heights.
Each breeze whispers jokes as it wanders by,
Tickling the leaves, making trees sigh.

Shadows play peek-a-boo with the sun,
While flowers roll over, just having fun.
Bumblebees buzzing, they wear tiny hats,
Making friends with daisies and even the cats.

In the quiet moments, a chorus of grins,
Where nature speaks softly, and everyone wins.
Grass grows mischievous, sprouting some glee,
As laughter erupts from a curl of a tree.

In this peaceful chaos, the colors collide,
A symphony woven where secrets abide.
And if you listen close, you'll hear them chime,
The echoes of joy that dance through the rhyme.

Secrets Beneath the Surface

Beneath the earth carpet, a party awaits,
With roots playing hopscotch and wormy debates.
Ladybugs giggle, they shuffle around,
In this underground realm, pure joy abounds.

A hidden domain where laughter can bloom,
With fungi in hats, making room for a room.
Gophers tell riddles to moles passing by,
While spiders weave tales that hang in the sky.

The rocks keep their wisdom, like old grumpy men,
They share tales of ages gone by, now and then.
Tunnels connect worlds, each twist and each turn,
Where silence can bubble and laughter can burn.

So tiptoe along where the whispers are deep,
For nature's clandestine, with secrets to keep.
In the heart of the earth, a chuckle or two,
In this joyous hideout, just waiting for you.

Nature's Gentle Confessions

In the garden, whispers play,
Petals giggle every day.
Roots are plotting quite a scheme,
To hide away in sunlight's beam.

Bumblebees wear tiny hats,
While ants parade like little brats.
The flowers wink as breezes tease,
Nature's secrets shared with ease.

A frog croaks jokes on lily pads,
While turtles stroll like old-time fads.
The sun bursts out in bright applause,
As flora laughs without a pause.

Confessions of the quiet woods,
In every nook, where mischief broods.
A leaf's soft chuckle in the air,
Nature's laughter everywhere.

Hushed Growth

In shadows deep, new life begins,
Grass creeps up, and the earth grins.
Mushrooms giggle in their spots,
While worms delight in tangled knots.

The wind, it hums a secret tune,
Tickling twigs beneath the moon.
Silent sprigs do a quiet dance,
Nature's laugh, it takes a chance.

A snail slips by with a sly smile,
Taking its time, going a mile.
The quietest blooms make the best jokes,
As laughter bursts from leafy folks.

In muted hues, humor thrives,
Nature's comic, in hush it strives.
Amidst the stillness, giggles soar,
In the garden, quiet galore.

Tranquil Awakening

Dawn creeps in on padded feet,
A sleepy bee becomes a greet.
Morning glories yawn and stretch,
Their soft petals, a playful sketch.

Squirrels chatter, playing tag,
While daisies blush, a friendly brag.
The pond reflects a grinning sun,
In peaceful jest, the day's begun.

Butterflies flit in endless glee,
Whispered tales of jubilee.
The turtle rolls in grass so fine,
With every giggle, they all shine.

In tranquil spots, the joy ignites,
Nature's laughter in the heights.
As the world wakes, it thrives and plays,
In quiet chuckles, through all the days.

The Sound of Softness

In the hush of twilight's glow,
The softest breezes start to flow.
Petals rustle, secrets bare,
Nature's whispers fill the air.

A sleepy fox slips through the trees,
Chasing shadows with playful ease.
The crickets sing their night-time tune,
Under the watch of the glowing moon.

Mice giggle in their cozy dens,
Joining in with nature's friends.
The nightingale hums a funny rhyme,
Tickling leaves, lost in time.

In the stillness, laughter swells,
In every nook, the magic dwells.
In the sounds of life's soft ways,
Nature's humor sings and plays.

Hidden Life Beneath

In the dark, the whispers grow,
Worms are dancing, putting on a show.
Rabbits giggle, grass tickles toes,
All beneath where no one knows.

A snail debates with a sleeping bee,
"Is life a race or just a spree?"
The roots conspire, plotting their fun,
Under the soil, where they've begun.

Mice in the shadows play hide and seek,
While mushrooms form a funky critique.
A ladybug winks, "This is my ground,"
And all around, laughter's the sound.

The earth is filled with secrets untold,
Where every critter is brave and bold.
So next time you walk, stoop down and peek,
At the hilarious lives hidden and meek.

Tenderness in the Wild

In the woods, the trees all sway,
A squirrel juggles nuts, what a display!
The birds chirp tunes, a comedic band,
While sunlight tickles the leafy stand.

A deer prances by with a dainty leap,
But trips on a twig, oh what a heap!
The laughter of nature echoes so bright,
As bushes blush with sheer delight.

A clever raccoon dons a sly disguise,
"Just a tree stump," he laughs, with twinkly eyes.
With every rustle, there's joy in the air,
In this wilderness fest, no room for despair.

So when you wander, just notice the play,
Of critters and blossoms in whimsical sway.
Nature's so funny, with each little scene,
In the wild, life's a big, chuckling dream.

The Calm Before the Blossoming

Beneath the frost, the stories stir,
As buds prepare in a soft, sweet blur.
"Will I be pink? Or maybe a blue?"
They muse in clusters, with laughter anew.

A daisy whispers to a sleepy rose,
"Oh dear friend, no one quite knows!"
While tulips gossip about colors and size,
In the hush of night, amid hidden ties.

A tiny sprout peeks through the snow,
"Hello, world! It's time for a show!"
As laughter ripples through the chilly air,
The buds chuckle, for spring's almost there.

So when winter warns with its chilly breath,
Remember the giggles that dance with death.
For in silence lies a symphony bright,
Waiting for warmth, to share in delight.

Secrets of the Seed

Deep in the soil, secrets abound,
Little ones giggle, no one makes a sound.
Each seed tells tales of dreams taking flight,
Clad in their shells, they hide out of sight.

A sunflower sips tea with a keen acorn,
"Why rush?" says one, "We'll rise with the dawn!"
With whispers of daisies spinning their tunes,
They scheme their designs 'neath the light of the moons.

Beans tell jokes that make cabbages laugh,
While carrots offer a witty giraffe.
In the stillness, hilarity grows,
As seeds chuckle softly, as everyone knows.

So next time you see dirt, just bend down to hear,
The humor of life that's hidden yet near.
Nature's punchlines, oh so discreet,
In the secrets of seeds, find the joy that's sweet.

A Whispered Invitation

In a corner of my mind, they play,
Tiny thoughts in a joyful ballet.
They tickle my brain, a giggly spree,
As I ponder on life's absurdity.

A squirrel winks and gives me a nudge,
While clouds hold their breath, refusing the sludge.
I glance at the sky, hoping for rain,
But it chuckles back, 'We're just playing !'

Quiet giggles dance on my cheek,
As laughter fairs beneath the peak.
Whispers flirt like butterflies bold,
Catching dreams in the air, untold.

So come join the fun, bring your cheer,
Let's revel in whispers that only we hear.
The world may be noisy, but we don't mind,
In our little haven, joy is unconfined.

Harmony in the Gloom

In shadows where giggles softly creep,
Silly secrets swirl, a playful leap.
Dancing like fireflies in the night,
Beneath the gloom, they sparkle and bite.

Whimsical frowns turn into smiles bright,
As sadness takes an unexpected flight.
A cat in a top hat prances about,
With a wink and a grin, 'What's this fuss about?'

In the corner, a lone shoe starts to sway,
It sings a tune in a funky ballet.
And in this quirky dance, we find grace,
Absurdity struts in the strangest place.

Join the jig in this wondrous dismay,
Where giggles abound, and worries decay.
In harmony, gloom surrenders its glee,
As laughter finds a way, just let it be.

Embraced by the Silence

Within the stillness, a whisper sneezes,
A random giggle that never ceases.
Silent snacks on memories sweet,
As time tiptoes in awkward defeat.

A rubber chicken flops on the floor,
Its honks echo softly, begging for more.
In the hush, alone but never quite,
We dance with shadows, a silly sight.

Quiet moments wrapped in mirth,
As giggling echoes give sound its worth.
The world holds its breath, but not for long,
For laughter sneaks in, a subtle song.

In this embrace, absurdity thrives,
Where whimsical thoughts do outrageous dives.
Let's waltz through whispers with playful glee,
Finding joy in the silence, just you and me.

Fragments of Stillness

In the quiet, a chuckle looms,
Like a jester hiding in darkened rooms.
Odd little bubbles of laughter burst,
Sprinkled confetti, a quirky thirst.

A penguin slips on a banana peel,
With a splash, it shows off its clumsy zeal.
In the fragments of stillness, joy is spread,
As curious whispers dance in my head.

Now a toaster hums a jazzy tune,
While spoons tap along, under the moon.
Each object a partner in this mad spree,
Shouting, 'Hey look! We're so fancy-free!'

Let's collect the giggles like fireflies bright,
In the pockets of stillness, a delightful sight.
Fragments of joy stitched tight in a seam,
In the dance of the quiet, we burst forth in dream.

Whispers in the Stillness

In the garden of a quiet mind,
Laughter blooms, though hard to find.
A butterfly dances, wings so wide,
Flapping gossip, secrets to confide.

A squirrel sneezes, the trees all shake,
A shush from the bushes, for goodness' sake!
Tickling silence, a comic parade,
Mischievous giggles in the shade.

The shadows giggle at the sun's bright glare,
Pretending they're busy, but they just don't care.
A frog gets the joke, leaps high in the air,
While crickets chuckle, as if they were aware.

In this stillness, paint your jokes with light,
Where whispers stretch and tickle the night.
The moon, a spectator, grins ear to ear,
While the stars share a laugh, "Oh dear, oh dear!"

Echoes of Unspoken Dreams

A dream flits by, all dressed in blue,
Hiding behind clouds that drift and skew.
It whispers softly, "I have a plan!"
But no one listens – just a feline scam.

The stars are giggling, twinkling bright,
Chatting in beams throughout the night.
"Did you see that wish?" one twinkles with glee,
"It just turned to spaghetti – oh, oh, can't you see?"

A tumbleweed rolls through the silent air,
With a funny hat and a wild flair.
It moves like it's dancing, all full of dreams,
Whispers and chuckles, bursting at the seams.

From dreams unspoken, laughter springs forth,
Funny little echoes of timeless worth.
As each twinkling wish takes its playful flight,
Who knew that dreaming could feel so light?

Buds of Quietude

Buds form boldly on the branches high,
They nod and wink, as clouds drift by.
A silent dance in the breeze's embrace,
While tress gossip gently with a leafy grace.

Mice play charades in a corner nook,
An acorn's role? A wise little book.
They read tales of cheese and faraway lands,
While squirrels are judging, making their stands.

In quietude, laughter secretly grows,
With whispers that tickle the tops of your toes.
Each little bud holds a punchline inside,
Taking the stage, nowhere to hide.

A bouquet of giggles, right under our noses,
Each bloom a comedian, mixing with roses.
So here's to the silence, where humor may leap,
In giggling gardens, where laughter can creep.

The Language of Unvoiced Thoughts

In the library of minds, thoughts silently play,
Puns hidden in pages, waiting all day.
A book sneezes softly, "Oh, what a plight!"
As another one whispers, "Just read me tonight!"

Laughter's a language that words cannot find,
In the heart of still waters, silliness unwinds.
Ink spills with giggles, beneath the quill's flight,
Each teardrop of joy, a splotch of delight.

Clouds hold the laughter, up high in the sky,
As they've mastered the art of the giggly sigh.
A rainbow forms jokes, bending colors to tease,
While raindrops chortle, as light as the breeze.

In the end, it's the silence that wraps us in cheer,
Whispering fun secrets for all who draw near.
So let's embrace quiet, with chuckles so true,
In a world of laughter, that's waiting for you.

Undercurrents of Tranquility

In a world that loves to chatter,
My cat's meow sounds like a clatter.
A squirrel sneezes, leaves start to shake,
Is nature laughing or a mistake?

Birds gossip softly on a wire,
Pigeons plotting, oh, they conspire.
A little breeze tickles the trees,
Nature's whispers make quite the tease.

The pond pretends it's a crystal ball,
Reflecting tales from trees so tall.
But what are those fish thinking, I wonder?
Why do they swim like they're in a blunder?

So hush now, let's hear the pranks unfold,
In the quiet, there's humor to behold.
Giggles and snickers in the breeze,
Nature's punchlines bring us to our knees.

The Unraveled Thread of Stillness

In the fabric of quiet, threads twine,
A mouse tips-toes, thinking it's fine.
A tumbleweed rolls, experiencing bliss,
While cacti chuckle, 'We've got this!'

Each leaf checks its watch, waits to drop,
But a beetle insists, 'No rush, let's hop!'
With frogs doing yoga on a lily pad,
It's obvious this stillness is a tad mad.

With silence thick enough to slice,
A worm whispers, 'I'm the quietest vice!'
And while the owl hoots of wisdom old,
The grass is green and stories are told.

Laughter in nature, hidden and sly,
A pause, a jiggle, passing birds fly.
So join the fun, keep it mute,
In tranquility's realm, all jesters suit!

Gentle Awakening

The sun peeks through, what a sight!
Roosters laugh, 'It's morning light!'
A snail does a stretch, oh what a grace,
While flowers yawn, taking their place.

Dewdrops giggle on petals green,
Calling bees for a breakfast scene.
A breeze teases, tickling each leaf,
As rabbits munch, with sly disbelief.

Every morning's an open mic,
Where crickets chirp, 'Hey, give it a hike!'
And ants march on, a parade of glee,
Joyful in their tiny esprit.

So rise with a chuckle, embrace the day,
The world is a canvas for laughter to play.
In the gentle wake of the sun's embrace,
Nature's comedy finds its space.

Blossoms of Reticence

In gardens quiet, secrets throng,
Whispers weave a funny song.
Petunias gossip, 'Did you see?
The daisies dance with glee and spree!'

Sunflowers nod, they're keeping tabs,
While worms are scheming like little brabs.
When shadows stretch, whispers grow,
Nature's humor, an undercover show.

A toad croaks jokes under the moon,
While fireflies blink, joining the tune.
The night is a canvas, laughter in the blue,
As quiet blooms bloom, bringing joy anew.

So here's to the shy, the soft and the meek,
They celebrate joy without a sneak peek.
In their stillness, a chuckle they lend,
For silence and humor, they beautifully blend!

Roots in the Void

In a garden where whispers play,
The veggies giggle at night and day.
Tomatoes dance with carrots in glee,
While radishes chant, 'Come laugh with me!'

A pumpkin joked, "Have you heard the news?"
"We've got no sound, but we've got great views!"
With roots that twist in a silent spree,
They plant the joy where none can see.

The lettuce lounges without a care,
While cucumbers float through the silent air.
A shy little onion starts to weep,
His tears, they sprout in the soil so deep!

But with each giggle beneath the ground,
The laughter booms, without a sound.
So next time you plant, remember this tale,
For in the quiet, hilarity prevails.

Quiet Blossoms

Beneath the stillness of the shade,
The flowers plot a funny parade.
Tulips twirl while daisies soar,
"Who knew silence could be such a roar?"

They speak in colors, a vivid talk,
With petals dancing in a sway and walk.
Roses chuckle in a rosy hue,
"Let's bloom together, it's what we do!"

Lilies whisper secrets to the bees,
"Zip it, boys, we're trying to tease!"
Violets wink and play hide and seek,
In this quiet world, the laughter peaks.

In the still of nature, mischief thrives,
With colors vibrant, the silence jives.
So check those blossoms next time you see,
For behind their calm, is pure glee!

Silenced Petals

In a field where sound took a nap,
Petals plotted their big ol' cap.
They twirled in hues, bright and far,
Joking, 'We're weird, but that's who we are!'

A sunflower stood with a tall, proud stance,
"Can you hear me?" he cried at a glance.
The breeze just chuckled, playing coy,
Silenced petals, but full of joy!

Daisies danced to a silent tune,
While buttercups swooned beneath the moon.
They shared the tales of their leafy plight,
Funny dreams hidden from plain sight.

In this garden of quiet delights,
Laughter blooms in the starry nights.
So when you look, don't just see the views,
Listen close—there's humor in their hues!

The Language of Growth

In the soil where whispers bloom,
The roots sit still, creating a room.
A seedling pokes through with a grin,
"Come join the fun, let's all begin!"

They chatter about sunshine's warm embrace,
Discussing the weather as part of the race.
"Let's stretch our leaves and show off our flair,
In the still air, we'll dance without care!"

The herbs gossip of fragrant ways,
In quiet spells of leafy plays.
Each twig and sprout has a tale to spin,
With laughter brewed in the roots within.

So here in the hush, joy does abound,
In silence, a symphony so profound.
Remember, each garden shares its own song,
In the stillness, we thrive and belong.

www.ingramcontent.com/pod-product-compliance
Lightning Source LLC
Chambersburg PA
CBHW072223070526
44585CB00015B/1462